STUDY GUIDE

LESTER SUMRALL TEACHING SERIES

DREAMS
AND
VISIONS

by
Dr. Lester Sumrall

LeSEA Publishing
530 E. Ireland Rd.
South Bend, IN 46614

www.leseapublishing.com

In this study guide, space is allowed for your personal notes so the text can grow into your own material.

Audios and videos for this series are available from LeSEA Publishing.

All scriptures, unless otherwise indicated, are taken from the *King James Version of the Holy Bible.*

Scriptures marked *NKJV* are taken from the *New King James Version of the Holy Bible.* Published by Thomas Nelson, Inc., Nashville, Tennessee, 1982.

DREAMS AND VISIONS OF HISTORY AND PROPHECY
ISBN 0-937580-78-3

This printing October 2016

Printed by LeSEA Publishing Co.
530 E. Ireland Rd.
South Bend, IN 46614

www.leseapublishing.com

STUDY GUIDE

LESTER SUMRALL TEACHING SERIES

DREAMS AND VISIONS

TABLE OF CONTENTS

STUDY GUIDE

LESTER SUMRALL TEACHING SERIES

DREAMS AND VISIONS

Lesson 1

AN INTRODUCTION TO DREAMS AND VISIONS

INTRODUCTION

The modern Church is often dubious of the supernatural, especially that which is manifested in dreams or visions. Christians are afraid of deceptions, counterfeits and spiritual misguidance.

Dreams and visions must be tested with spiritual leadership, just like spiritual gifts. Prophetically, the time has come for many remarkable manifestations of the supernatural. Only people who are spiritually in tune will understand the message.

READING

I Corinthians 14:29, *Let the prophets speak two or three, and let the other judge.*

1. GOD PROMISED HIS PEOPLE

God spoke to Moses, Aaron and Miriam.

Numbers 12:6, *And he said, Hear now my words: If there be a prophet among you, I the LORD will make myself known unto him in a vision, and will speak unto him in a dream.*

2. THIS IS THE HOUR OF THE SUPERNATURAL

A. Throughout the historic annals of humanity, no other generation has been as strongly involved with the supernatural as this one. The supernatural is a sign of the last days.

B. The modern world is preparing for the mysteries of outer space and interstellar transportation through movies, television, books and magazines.

C. These studies are imperative because the political, religious and social systems of the end-time will function within the realm of the supernatural.

3. THE CHURCH IN PROPHECY

Dreams and visions are for today.

Joel 2:28, *And it shall come to pass afterward, that I will pour out my spirit upon all flesh; and your sons and your daughters shall prophesy, your old men shall dream dreams, your young men shall see visions.*

4. SUPERNATURAL EVENTS

Dreams and visions fall into the category of supernatural events. Much of biblical and secular history is amazingly related to visions, dreams and prophecy. From Genesis to Revelation, remarkable visions and dreams direct the course of human destiny.

Biblical dreams and visions are supernatural in origin and essence. They are revelatory in significance. We must relate to them spiritually.

5. THE PROS AND CONS

A. In this present world system there are arguments for and against dreams and visions.

Some intellectuals consider dreams and visions to be phantoms of the night. They teach that no special significance should be given to them. They believe visions and dreams are caused by such things as emotional stress, physical illness or gluttony.

B. At the other extreme, there are people who direct their lives with some form of supernatural revelation.

The devil takes advantage of this mental attitude and tries to destroy these people with lies.

There is a center of the road which is verifiable by the Body of Christ, and in these studies I seek to relate to truth.

6. THE DIFFERENCES BETWEEN DREAMS, VISIONS, AND TRANCES

A. During a dream you are asleep. Sleep is a function of the human brain. It is a subliminal function. Most dreams are natural and have no spiritual significance at all.

B. During a vision the person is awake. Again it is a mental function; the person sees an image with brain waves and not the physical eye.

Numbers 24:16, *He hath said, which heard the words of God, and knew the knowledge of the most High, which saw the vision of the Almighty, falling into a trance, but having his eyes open:*

C. During a dream-revelation, or trance, the person is not awake or alert, but in a subliminal attitude. The individual has his or her natural eyes open and is aware of his mental abilities or senses.

7. TWO WORLDS

There are two worlds for humans to live in—the *awake* world and the *sleep* world; the day world and the night world.

Dreams and visions both occur in the area of the sleep world. At this point the individual is motionless. His eyes can be either open or closed. His attention is fully attuned to the phenomenon. There are many different kinds of dreams and visions.

A. During dreams, the subliminal mind undergoes a sequence of sensations. Images or thoughts pass through the sleeping person's brain.

B. During a vision, a person sees with something other than normal eyesight. It is supernaturally revealed information.

C. A trance is a stunned or dazed condition of mental abstraction. It resembles sleep, but the person is receiving information supernaturally.

D. Balaam, one of the strangest prophets in history spoke about a trance:

Numbers 24:4, *He hath said, which heard the words of God, which saw the vision of the Almighty, falling into a trance, but having his eyes open.*

E. The apostle Peter also experienced this phenomenon.

Acts 10:10, *And he became very hungry, and would have eaten: but while they made ready, he fell into a trance.*

F. Paul testified to a trance experience in Jerusalem.

Acts 22:17, *And it came to pass, that, when I was come again to Jerusalem, even while I prayed in the temple, I was in a trance;*

8. PAUL HAD VISIONS

God is omniscient and can reveal knowledge in any form He chooses.

A. Paul, first known as Saul, received a vision near the city of Damascus.

> Acts 9:1-5, *And Saul, yet breathing out threatenings and slaughter against the disciples of the Lord, went unto the high priest,*
> v. 2, *And desired of him letters to Damascus to the synagogues, that if he found any of this way, whether they were men or women, he might bring them bound unto Jerusalem.*
> v. 3, *And as he journeyed, he came near Damascus: and suddenly there shined round about him a light from heaven:*
> v. 4, *And he fell to the earth, and heard a voice saying unto him, Saul, Saul, why persecutest thou me?*
> v. 5, *And he said, Who art thou, Lord? And the Lord said, I am Jesus whom thou persecutest: it is hard for thee to kick against the pricks.*

B. Paul was sent to Macedonia through a night vision.

> Acts 16:9, *And a vision appeared to Paul in the night; There stood a man of Macedonia, and prayed him, saying, Come over into Macedonia, and help us.*

> Acts 26:19, *...I was not disobedient unto the heavenly vision:*

9. PETER FELL INTO A TRANCE AND HAD A VISION

> Acts 11:1-10, *And the apostles and brethren that were in Judaea heard that the Gentiles had also received the word of God.*
> v. 2, *And when Peter was come up to Jerusalem, they that were of the circumcision contended with him,*
> v. 3, *Saying, Thou wentest in to men uncircumcised, and didst eat with them.*
> v. 4, *But Peter rehearsed the matter from the beginning, and expounded it by order unto them, saying,*
> v. 5, *I was in the city of Joppa praying: and in a trance I saw a vision, A certain vessel descend, as it had been a great sheet, let down from heaven by four corners; and it came even to me:*
> v. 6, *Upon the which when I had fastened mine eyes, I considered, and saw four-footed beasts of the earth, and wild beasts, and creeping things, and fowls of the air.*
> v. 7, *And I heard a voice saying unto me, Arise, Peter; slay and eat.*
> v. 8, *But I said, Not so, Lord: for nothing common or unclean hath at any time entered into my mouth.*
> v. 9, *But the voice answered me again from heaven, What God hath cleansed, that call not thou common.*
> v. 10, *And this was done three times: and all were drawn up again into heaven.*

10. HEBREW WORDS FOR DREAMS AND VISIONS

The Old Testament uses several words which are translated as dream or vision. Here are a few of those words.

A. *Chazown* means "mental sight or revelation through mental seeing."

    1) This could come in the form of a divine utterance as in:

    Daniel 9:24, *Seventy weeks are determined upon thy people and upon thy holy city, to finish the transgression, and to make an end of sins, and to make reconciliation for iniquity, and to bring in everlasting righteousness, and to seal up the vision and prophecy, and to anoint the most Holy.*

    2) In Samuel's time, there was no open vision.

    I Samuel 3:1, *And the child Samuel ministered unto the LORD before Eli. And the word of the LORD was precious in those days; there was no open vision.*

B. *Chalom* means "dream."

Daniel 2:1-2, *And in the second year of the reign of Nebuchadnezzar Nebuchadnezzar dreamed dreams, wherewith his spirit was troubled, and his sleep brake from him.*
v. 2, *Then the king commanded to call the magicians, and the astrologers, and the sorcerers, and the Chaldeans, for to show the king his dreams. So they came and stood before the king.*

C. *Chelem* means "dream."

Daniel 2:4-6, *Then spake the Chaldeans to the king in Syriack, O king, live for ever: tell thy servants the dream, and we will show the interpretation.*
v. 5, *The king answered and said to the Chaldeans, The thing is gone from me: if ye will not make known unto me the dream, with the interpretation thereof, ye shall be cut in pieces, and your houses shall be made a dunghill.*
v. 6, *But if ye show the dream, and the interpretation thereof, ye shall receive of me gifts and rewards and great honor: therefore show me the dream, and the interpretation thereof.*

D. *Marah* means "a vision as seeing something in a mirror; appearance."

Daniel 8:16, 26-27, *And I heard a man's voice between the banks of Ulai, which called, and said, Gabriel, make this man to understand the vision.*

v. 26, *And the vision of the evening and the morning which was told is true: wherefore shut thou up the vision; for it shall be for many days.*
v. 27, *And I Daniel fainted, and was sick certain days; afterward I rose up, and did the king's business; and I was astonished at the vision, but none understood it.*

One of the signs of Christ's return will be an increase in the spiritual phenomena of supernatural dreams and visions.

STUDY GUIDE

LESTER SUMRALL TEACHING SERIES

DREAMS AND VISIONS

Lesson 2

DOES GOD COMMUNICATE THROUGH DREAMS AND VISIONS?

INTRODUCTION

Throughout history, God has spoken to people through supernatural dreams and visions.

Today many people have overlooked this avenue of communication, but God is still willing to use it. As we enter the last days, dreams and visions will become even more important to the Church.

Dreams are a mystery to modern science. They do not know what causes dreams.

1. **GOD THE GREAT COMMUNICATOR**

   God has communicated with individuals for over 6,000 years.

   A. God walked with Adam.

   B. Enoch walked with God.

   C. God talked to Abraham. He ate with him.

   D. God communicated with Moses face to face.

   E. Divine prophecy can come through dreams or visions. A person will know it is from God because the dream will come true. God's plan of the ages was recorded because of dreams and visions. From Genesis to Revelation, God revealed Himself with special dreams while man slept.

      God has manifested Himself and supernaturally revealed things unseen by the natural eye through dreams and visions.

11

F. All kinds of people have experienced supernatural visions from God. Many of these dreams contained messages from God.

Job 33:14-18, *For God speaketh once, yea twice, yet man perceiveth it not.*
v. 15, *In a dream, in a vision of the night, when deep sleep falleth upon men, in slumberings upon the bed;*
v. 16, *Then he openeth the ears of men, and sealeth their instruction,*
v. 17, *That he may withdraw man from his purpose, and hide pride from man.*
v. 18, *He keepeth back his soul from the pit, and his life from perishing by the sword.*

The book of Job is considered one of the oldest books in the world. It demonstrates divine purposes for God using dreams and visions.

2. **KINGS HAVE BEEN LED WITH DREAMS AND VISIONS**

A. Abimelech

Genesis 20:3, *But God came to Abimelech in a dream by night, and said to him, Behold, thou art but a dead man, for the woman which thou hast taken; for she is a man's wife.*

This dream was given to keep a king from committing adultery and destroying his life.

Abraham's wife, Sarah, was preserved from moral contamination. The seed of the promised Messiah was saved. God did all this through a dream.

B. Pharaoh

Genesis 41:15-24, *And Pharaoh said unto Joseph, I have dreamed a dream, and there is none that can interpret it: and I have heard say of thee, that thou canst understand a dream to interpret it.*
v. 16, *And Joseph answered Pharaoh, saying, It is not in me: God shall give Pharaoh an answer of peace.*
v. 17, *And Pharaoh said unto Joseph, In my dream, behold, I stood upon the bank of the river:*
v. 18, *And, behold, there came up out of the river seven kine, fat fleshed and well favored; and they fed in a meadow:*
v. 19, *And, behold, seven other kine came up after them, poor and very ill favored and lean fleshed, such as I never saw in all the land of Egypt for badness:*
v. 20, *And the lean and the ill favored kine did eat up the first seven fat kine:*
v. 21, *And when they had eaten them up, it could not be known that they had eaten them; but they were still ill favored, as at the beginning. So I awoke.*
v. 22, *And I saw in my dream, and, behold, seven ears came up in one stalk, full and good:*

v. 23, *And, behold, seven ears, withered, thin, and blasted with the east wind, sprung up after them:*
v. 24, *And the thin ears devoured the seven good ears: and I told this unto the magicians; but there was none that could declare it to me.*

C. Nebuchadnezzar

Daniel 2:1, *Now in the second year of Nebuchadnezzar's reign, Nebuchadnezzar had dreams; and his spirit was so troubled that his sleep left him.* (NKJV)

D. Isaiah ministered to kings through visions.

Isaiah 1:1, *The vision of Isaiah the son of Amoz, which he saw concerning Judah and Jerusalem in the days of Uzziah, Jotham, Ahaz, and Hezekiah, kings of Judah.*

E. Nahum had a vision for a nation.

Nahum 1:1, *The burden of Nineveh. The book of the vision of Nahum the Elkoshite.*

F. Daniel had a vision of the future.

Daniel 8:1-2, 13-17, *In the third year of the reign of king Belshazzar a vision appeared unto me, even unto me Daniel, after that which appeared unto me at the first.*
v. 2, *And I saw in a vision; and it came to pass, when I saw, that I was at Shushan in the palace, which is in the province of Elam; and I saw in a vision, and I was by the river of Ulai.*

v. 13, *Then I heard one saint speaking, and another saint said unto that certain saint which spake, How long shall be the vision concerning the daily sacrifice, and the transgression of desolation, to give both the sanctuary and the host to be trodden under foot?*
v. 14, *And he said unto me, Unto two thousand and three hundred days; then shall the sanctuary be cleansed.*
v. 15, *And it came to pass, when I, even I Daniel, had seen the vision, and sought for the meaning, then, behold, there stood before me as the appearance of a man.*
v. 16, *And I heard a man's voice between the banks of Ulai, which called, and said, Gabriel, make this man to understand the vision.*
v. 17, *So he came near where I stood: and when he came, I was afraid, and fell upon my face: but he said unto me, Understand, O son of man: for at the time of the end shall be the vision.*

3. PROPHECY IS THE GREATEST MINISTRY OF DREAMS AND VISIONS

Dreams and visions deal with the miraculous. God wants to reveal Himself to man, and one way He does this is through dreams and visions.

A vision is a scene God wants you to see. It can be a past event He brings to light. It can be something happening in the present. It can be a revelation of the future or prophecy.

Dreams and visions often have to do with God's relationship to an individual, city or nation.

4. JACOB

While Jacob was a vagabond from home, he dreamt that a ladder came down from heaven with angels ascending and descending on it. This dream gave Jacob the assurance that God was with him to protect him.

Genesis 28:10-16, *And Jacob went out from Beersheba, and went toward Haran.*
v. 11, *And he lighted upon a certain place, and tarried there all night, because the sun was set; and he took of the stones of that place, and put them for his pillows, and lay down in that place to sleep.*
v. 12, *And he dreamed, and behold a ladder set up on the earth, and the top of it reached to heaven: and behold the angels of God ascending and descending on it.*
v. 13, *And, behold, the LORD stood above it, and said, I am the LORD God of Abraham thy father, and the God of Isaac: the land whereon thou liest, to thee will I give it, and to thy seed;*
v. 14, *And thy seed shall be as the dust of the earth, and thou shalt spread abroad to the west, and to the east, and to the north, and to the south: and in thee and in thy seed shall all the families of the earth be blessed.*
v. 15, *And, behold, I am with thee, and will keep thee in all places whither thou goest, and will bring thee again into this land; for I will not leave thee, until I have done that which I have spoken to thee of.*
v. 16, *And Jacob awaked out of his sleep, and he said, Surely the LORD is in this place; and I knew it not.*

Jacob identified God with the place or area. He named it Bethel which means *house of God.* It later became a prominent town in the Bible.

Jacob covenanted to become a faithful tither. He gave ten percent of his income throughout the rest of his life.

5. SOME DREAMS AND VISIONS RECORDED IN THE BIBLE

A. Abimelech

Genesis 20:3, *But God came to Abimelech in a dream by night, and said to him, Behold, thou art but a dead man, for the woman which thou hast taken; for she is a man's wife.*

B. God revealed to Jacob which cattle would make him rich.

Genesis 31:10-13, *And it came to pass at the time that the cattle conceived, that I lifted up mine eyes, and saw in a dream, and, behold, the rams which leaped upon the cattle were ring-streaked, speckled, and grisled..*
v. 11, *And the angel of God spake unto me in a dream, saying, Jacob: And I said, Here am I.*
v. 12, *And he said, Lift up now thine eyes, and see, all the rams which leap upon the cattle are ring-streaked, speckled, and grisled: for I have seen all that Laban doeth unto thee.*
v. 13, *I am the God of Bethel, where thou anointedst the pillar, and where thou vowedst a vow unto me: now arise, get thee out from this land, and return unto the land of thy kindred.*

C. God spoke to Laban.

Genesis 31:24, *And God came to Laban the Syrian in a dream by night, and said unto him, Take heed that thou speak not to Jacob either good or bad.*

D. Joseph had dreams when he was 17 years old.

Genesis 37:5, *And Joseph dreamed a dream, and he told it his brethren: and they hated him yet the more.*

E. Joseph dreamed about his mother and father.

Genesis 37:9, *And he dreamed yet another dream, and told it his brethren, and said, Behold, I have dreamed a dream more; and, behold, the sun and the moon and the eleven stars made obeisance to me.*

F. A pagan butler and baker.

1) Genesis 40:9, *And the chief butler told his dream to Joseph, and said to him, In my dream, behold, a vine was before me.*

2) Genesis 40:16, *When the chief baker saw that the interpretation was good, he said unto Joseph, I also was in my dream, and, behold, I had three white baskets on my head.*

G. The king of Egypt dreamed.

Genesis 41:1-8, *And it came to pass at the end of two full years, that Pharaoh dreamed: and, behold, he stood by the river.*

v. 2, *And, behold, there came up out of the river seven well favored kine and fat fleshed; and they fed in a meadow.*

v. 3, *And, behold, seven other kine came up after them out of the river, ill favored and lean fleshed; and stood by the other kine upon the brink of the river.*

v. 4, *And the ill favored and lean fleshed kine did eat up the seven well favored and fat kine. So Pharaoh awoke.*

v. 5, *And he slept and dreamed the second time: and, behold, seven ears of corn came up upon one stalk, rank and good.*

v. 6, *And, behold, seven thin ears and blasted with the east wind sprung up after them.*

v. 7, *And the seven thin ears devoured the seven rank and full ears. And Pharaoh awoke, and, behold, it was a dream.*

v. 8, *And it came to pass in the morning that his spirit was troubled; and he sent and called for all the magicians of Egypt, and all the wise men thereof: and Pharaoh told them his dream; but there was none that could interpret them unto Pharaoh.*

H. Solomon gained wisdom through a dream.

I Kings 3:3-15, *And Solomon loved the LORD, walking in the statutes of David his father: only he sacrificed and burnt incense in high places.*

v. 4, *And the king went to Gibeon to sacrifice there; for that was the great high place: a thousand burnt offerings did Solomon offer upon that altar.*

v. 5, *In Gibeon the LORD appeared to Solomon in a dream by night: and God said, Ask what I shall give thee.*

v. 6, *And Solomon said, Thou hast showed unto thy servant David my father great mercy, according as he walked before thee in truth, and in righteousness, and in uprightness of heart with thee; and thou hast kept for him this great kindness, that thou hast given him a son to sit on his throne, as it is this day.*

v. 7, *And now, O LORD my God, thou hast made thy servant king instead of David my father: and I am but a little child: I know not how to go out or come in.*

v. 8, *And thy servant is in the midst of thy people which thou hast chosen, a great people, that cannot be numbered nor counted for multitude.*

v. 9, *Give therefore thy servant an understanding heart to judge thy people, that I may discern between good and bad: for who is able to judge this thy so great a people?*

v. 10, *And the speech pleased the Lord, that Solomon had asked this thing.*

v. 11, *And God said unto him, Because thou hast asked this thing, and hast not asked for thyself long life; neither hast asked riches for thyself, nor hast asked the life of thine enemies; but hast asked for thyself understanding to discern judgment;*

v. 12, *Behold, I have done according to thy words: lo, I have given thee a wise and an understanding heart; so that there was none like thee before thee, neither after thee shall any arise like unto thee.*

v. 13, *And I have also given thee that which thou hast not asked, both riches, and honor: so that there shall not be any among the kings like unto thee all thy days.*

v. 14, *And if thou wilt walk in my ways, to keep my statutes and my commandments, as thy father David did walk, then I will lengthen thy days.*

v. 15, *And Solomon awoke; and, behold, it was a dream. And he came to Jerusalem, and stood before the ark of the covenant of the LORD, and offered up burnt offerings, and offered peace offerings, and made a feast to all his servants.*

I. The book of Job.

1) Job 4:12-21, *Now a thing was secretly brought to me, and mine ear received a little thereof.*
v. 13, *In thoughts from the visions of the night, when deep sleep falleth on men,*
v. 14, *Fear came upon me, and trembling, which made all my bones to shake.*
v. 15, *Then a spirit passed before my face; the hair of my flesh stood up:*
v. 16, *It stood still, but I could not discern the form thereof: an image was before mine eyes, there was silence, and I heard a voice, saying,*
v. 17, *Shall mortal man be more just than God? shall a man be more pure than his maker?*
v. 18, *Behold, he put no trust in his servants; and his angels he charged with folly:*
v. 19, *How much less in them that dwell in houses of clay, whose foundation is in the dust, which are crushed before the moth?*
v. 20, *They are destroyed from morning to evening: they perish for ever without any regarding it.*
v. 21, *Doth not their excellency which is in them go away? they die, even without wisdom.*

2) Job 7:14, *Then thou scarest me with dreams, and terrifiest me through visions:*

J. Historical false prophets had false dreams.

1) Jeremiah 23:29-32, *Is not my word like as a fire? saith the LORD; and like a hammer that breaketh the rock in pieces?*
v. 30, *Therefore, behold, I am against the prophets, saith the LORD, that steal my words every one from his neighbor.*
v. 31, *Behold, I am against the prophets, saith the LORD, that use their tongues, and say, He saith.*
v. 32, *Behold, I am against them that prophesy false dreams, saith the LORD, and do tell them, and cause my people to err by their lies, and by their lightness; yet I sent them not, nor commanded them: therefore they shall not profit this people at all, saith the LORD.*

2) Jeremiah 29:8, *For thus says the LORD of hosts, the God of Israel: Do not let your prophets and your diviners who are in your midst deceive you, nor listen to your dreams which you cause to be dreamed.* (NKJV)

K. Joseph, the husband of the virgin Mary, was directed by dreams.

1) Joseph accepted the birth of Christ because of a dream.

Matthew 1:20, *But while he thought on these things, behold, the angel of the Lord appeared unto him in a dream, saying, Joseph, thou son of David, fear not to take unto thee Mary thy wife: for that which is conceived in her is of the Holy Ghost.*

2) Joseph and Mary were warned to flee to Egypt through a dream.

Matthew 2:13, *And when they were departed, behold, the angel of the Lord appeareth to Joseph in a dream, saying, Arise, and take the young child and his mother, and flee into Egypt, and be thou there until I bring thee word: for Herod will seek the young child to destroy him.*

3) Joseph knew about Herod's death through a dream.

Matthew 2:19, *But when Herod was dead, behold, an angel of the Lord appeareth in a dream to Joseph in Egypt,*

4) Joseph moved to Galilee because of a dream.

Matthew 2:22, *But when he heard that Archelaus did reign in Judaea in the room of his father Herod, he was afraid to go thither: notwithstanding, being warned of God in a dream, he turned aside into the parts of Galilee.*

L. The wise men redirected their journey because of a dream.

Matthew 2:12, *And being warned of God in a dream that they should not return to Herod, they departed into their own country another way.*

M. The Bible concludes with John's vision of Christ.

Revelation 1:12-18, *And I turned to see the voice that spake with me. And being turned, I saw seven golden candlesticks;*
v. 13, *And in the midst of the seven candlesticks one like unto the Son of man, clothed with a garment down to the foot, and girt about the paps with a golden girdle.*
v. 14, *His head and his hairs were white like wool, as white as snow; and his eyes were as a flame of fire;*
v. 15, *And his feet like unto fine brass, as if they burned in a furnace; and his voice as the sound of many waters.*
v. 16, *And he had in his right hand seven stars: and out of his mouth went a sharp two-edged sword: and his countenance was as the sun shineth in his strength.*

v. 17, *And when I saw him, I fell at his feet as dead. And he laid his right hand upon me, saying unto me, Fear not; I am the first and the last:*
v. 18, *I am he that liveth, and was dead; and, behold, I am alive for evermore, Amen; and have the keys of hell and of death.*

N. This is a short list of how the Almighty has bypassed man's normal, human faculties in order to communicate outside of the body experiences. This is God's way of assuring man that the information received is not of human origin.

STUDY GUIDE

LESTER SUMRALL TEACHING SERIES

DREAMS AND VISIONS

Lesson 3

DREAMS VS. TRANCES

INTRODUCTION

Dreams and visions are as universal as humanity. Unholy, secular visions and dreams of mankind are well documented.

The occult world and non-evangelical church bodies have written about dreams and visions in books and pamphlets. The Bible instructs Christians to beware of them.

Pagans frequently see the demon world. Grotesque gods of anger, revenge and hate have been seen in visions. Sculptures and paintings are often made to resemble these deities.

An idol in the Rajah's palace in Java had 50 arms and hands. I talked to the priest who fabricated it. He had seen the god in a mysterious vision and modeled it from that vision. I told him the difference between his god and my God was that I worshiped the Creator, and he worshiped part of God's creation.

READING

Galatians 1:8-9, *But though we, or an angel from heaven, preach any other gospel unto you than that which we have preached unto you, let him be accursed.*
v. 9, *As we said before, so say I now again, If any man preach any other gospel unto you than that ye have received, let him be accursed.*

1. DEVILISH DREAMS

    A. Jude 1:8, *Likewise also these filthy dreamers defile the flesh, despise dominion, and speak evil of dignities.*

    B. Deuteronomy 13:5, *And that prophet, or that dreamer of dreams, shall be put to death; because he hath spoken to turn you away from the LORD your God, which brought you out of the land of Egypt, and redeemed you out of the house of bondage, to thrust thee* *out of the way which the LORD thy God commanded thee to walk in. So shalt thou put the evil away from the midst of thee.*

C. The devil can use a dream or vision. Non-Christian religions are often based upon fantasies of hallucinations and trances. Most cults are built on a private revelation.

1) Egyptians and Babylonians

Both the Egyptian and Babylonian religions were based on visions and dreams.

2) Buddhists

Buddha was a religious leader named Siddhartha Gautama. He lived simultaneously with Zechariah and Malachi for 31 years.

He was born in 563 B.C. He received his vision or enlightenment while sitting under a bodhi tree. Buddha sought *nirvana*, the ideal state of peace, by practicing yoga and mind control.[1]

3) Moslems

Mohammedanism, or Islam, started from the mystic visions of a camel driver named Ubu-el-Kassim, later known as Mohammed. He was born in Mecca in 570 A.D.

According to Islamic tradition, when he was 40 he entered the Hira cave and was met by a being who identified itself as the angel Gabriel. This being choked Mohammed into submission and declared, "Proclaim in the name of the Lord the Creator who created man from a clot of blood."

During later visits to the same cave, Mohammed received more revelations. What he saw and heard was summarized in the Koran, Islam's sacred book. During a 22-year period, Mohammed memorized all 78,000 words of the Koran's 114 chapters. Since he was illiterate, he taught about his visions orally.[2]

Islam equates Mohammed with the Lord Jesus Christ. It teaches that there are seven great leaders chosen by God; among them were Abraham, Moses, Mohammed and Adam.

---

[1] Larson, Bob. <u>Larson's Book of Cults</u>. (Wheaton, IL: Tyndale House Publishers Inc., 1984), pp. 83-84.

[2] Larson, pp. 103-104.

4) The Mormons

The Church of Jesus Christ Of Latter Day Saints, also called Mormonism, was founded by Joseph Smith. In 1820, he had a vision while he was in the woods praying. In this vision, he claimed that God the Father and God the Son materialized and spoke to him.[3]

According to Smith, the Father and the Son took a rather dim view of the Christian church and of the world in general. Announcing that a restoration of true Christianity was needed, they appointed Joseph Smith to launch the new dispensation.

Mormonism is based not on the Bible, but on a "new revelation." This is against the Word of God. Valid dreams and visions have to be according to that which can already be found in the Bible.

5) The Church Of The New Jerusalem/Swedenborgianism

Emanuel Swedenborg considered himself a seer of a new revelation from God, which superseded the interpretational powers of the church fathers and the reformers. He was preoccupied with dreams, visions and alleged messages from and conversations with spirits and the spirit world.[4]

6) The Unification Church/Moonies

Sun Myung Moon is the founder of the Unification Church. He was born in Korea in 1920. Moon claims to have received a vision of Christ in 1936. This vision told him that he must finish the work started by Christ. His followers believe Moon to be the Messiah, the Lord of the Second Advent. According to the Unification Church, the book, <u>Divine Principle</u>, is the completed testament, and supersedes the Bible. It contains spiritual truth for this age which has not been revealed previously.[5]

7) Jeane Dixon

Jeane Dixon has been an unofficial advisor to presidents, prime ministers, congressmen and other dignitaries, because of her claim to a prophetic gift. Each morning, Jeane Dixon "asks God" to reveal anything to her which would enlighten

---

[3] Larson, pp. 157-158.

[4] Larson, pp. 396-397.

[5] Larson, pp. 224-226.

and better mankind. These revelations come to Jeane Dixon through a great variety of ways. When these means of communication are examined, a veritable occultist's complete bag of tricks is discovered.

She uses such methods as visions, crystal ball, astrology, numerology, dreams, tarot cards, inner voices, mental telepathy, and finger touching for the reception of revelatory information.

Jeane Dixon foresaw a world holocaust in the 1980s. Ruth Montgomery wrote in her book, A Gift of Prophecy:

> After this period, she forecasts that Rome will once again become the world's foremost center of culture, learning, and religion; and that the Middle Eastern child whose birth she "witnessed in the vision with Queen Nefertiti" on February 5, 1962, will untie all warring creeds and sects into one all-embracing faith.[6]

8) Edgar Cayce—The Sleeping Prophet

Today, there is great interest in the supernatural and the metaphysical—a realm above and beyond sense experience. Parapsychology, astrology, prophecy, Atlantis, and reincarnation are generating a great deal of excitement through various media.

The late Edgar Cayce, whose readings are still very popular today, is an outstanding example of the above. "A reading" is a term used to describe the clairvoyant discourses which Edgar Cayce gave while in a self-induced hypnotic sleep-state. His work is carried on by The Association for Research and Enlightenment (ARE) in Virginia Beach, Virginia, as well as numerous ARE study groups located throughout the United States.

9) The Temple of Pa in Singapore

A fortune-teller was in a trance in the temple foyer. She wrote with her eyes closed

---

[6] Montgomery, Ruth. A Gift of Prophecy. (New York: William Morrown and Company, 1965), p. 182.

and did not even know what she had written. People paid to have their fortunes told. Her revelations were supernatural, but they were not from God.

2. DREAMS VS. VISIONS

A. Dreams are born during sleep.

    1) Psalm 4:8, *I will both lay me down in peace, and sleep: for thou, LORD, only makest me dwell in safety.*

    2) Psalm 127:2, *It is vain for you to rise up early, to sit up late, to eat the bread of sorrows: for so he giveth his beloved sleep.*

    3) Proverbs 3:24, *When thou liest down, thou shalt not be afraid: yea, thou shalt lie down, and thy sleep shall be sweet.*

B. Trances are a day operation. Oftentimes the natural eyes are open while one "sees" a vision of a person, place or thing.

3. DREAMS IN THE NIGHT

A person must be in a state of sleep in order to have a dream. They occur mostly during Rapid Eye Movement (REM) sleep.

A. Greek word for sleep is *hypno*. We also get the words, hypnotic and hypnosis from this Greek term.

B. Humans spend one third of their lives sleeping.

C. 32% of Americans suffer from insomnia.

D. Millions of Americans have severe sleeping problems. They take tons of medicine in order to sleep.

4. HUMAN SLEEP

A. God neither slumbers nor sleeps.

Psalm 121:4, *Behold, he that keepeth Israel shall neither slumber nor sleep.*

B. In eternity no one sleeps.

Revelation 21:25, *And the gates of it shall not be shut at all by day: for there shall be no night there.*

C.   Human sleep has been called "the unknown cosmos." Each night humans, like Christopher Columbus, sail forth to discover a new world. We prepare for a voyage into the night. Some of these voyages are very complicated.

D.   Humans live their lives by *circadian*, a Latin word for "around the day." This means humans live by the planetary movement of the earth around the sun. Man is essentially a creature of day. His opposite are diurnal, or nocturnal animals such as bats, cats and owls, which are awake at night and sleep in the day.

E.   Human sleep possesses the elements of time, space, sensation and restoration. Sleep can turn back time, move from continent to continent, and create amazing sensations. It restores human strength.

F.   During sleep we depart the world of people, objects, colors and action to a private and inward world of self.

5.   DREAMS CAN REVEAL SECRETS

A.   Troubled persons express their conflict in their body language while they sleep.

B.   Our sleep world is full of signs and signals that indicate the direction of our life.

C.   Our fears and hates or our loves and joys are revealed in our sleep and sleep positions. Even our personalities are revealed by the way we sleep.

D.   Our hands, eyes and feet are articulate during sleep.

E.   When one's life is bent out of shape, his body in the dark will virtually tie itself up to describe the twists and turns of his waking life.

6.   SOME PEOPLE FEAR SLEEP

A.   Millions of people are afraid to sleep. Some fear they will never wake up again.

B.   Some spiritualists teach that the soul of man wanders while he sleeps. Others teach that the soul becomes another form when he sleeps.

7.   CHANGING YOUR SLEEP POSITIONS

It has been said that:

The king sleeps upon his back.

The wise man sleeps upon his side.

The rich man sleeps upon his stomach.

When a person becomes a Christian, his sleep pattern changes. If he is aggressive or repressive, it changes.

If a person has been through great sorrow and depression, he will sleep curled up into a knot. This automatically changes with a victorious position in Christ.

8. THE CHRISTIAN'S SLEEP

    A. Psalm 127:2, *...he giveth his beloved sleep.*

    B. Proverbs 3:24, *When thou liest down, thou shalt not be afraid: yea, thou shalt lie down, and thy sleep shall be sweet.*

    God gives His own sweet peace from fear.

9. MY DREAM

Everyday, I leave a television audience of thousands. I leave guests and television workers to go home to my family. Then from the family and a house full of rooms, I go to one room, then to one bed and sleep. This is the narrowing of activities. We restrict our attention and turn inward from world conditions, to family, to self. This means, in order to sleep, our lives change from a vertical situation to a horizontal perspective. We shift from public to private and personal life space.

10. FACTS ABOUT SLEEP

    A. Dreams usually occur in black and white, not color.

    B. During sleep we see with our thoughts while our minds drift and remain active.

    C. Sleep is unique in that we lose the confinements of space. We often fly or find ourselves in a foreign land. We lose the confinement of time and become a child again. We lose the confinement of energy and can do impossible things.

        1) Fantasy Dreams

        A child may dream about riding wild horses, and even act out the ride in his sleep.

        2) Memory Dreams

        These dreams concern events a person remembers from his or her past.

3) Spiritual Dreams

These dreams are the greatest when God speaks to us about spiritual matters—of growing in God and increasing in God.

4) Prophetic Dreams

God can show us things that will come to pass in the future.

11. THE FOUR STAGES OF SLEEP

A. Theta

Heart and breathing slow down. Outside activities diminish.

B. K Complex

Sleep spindles and eyes become still. This stage lasts about five minutes.

C. Delta

Heart and breathing rates are 30 percent lower than waking hours.

D. REM (Rapid Eye Movement)

Heartbeat increases and dreams are vivid and emotionally active.

STUDY GUIDE

LESTER SUMRALL TEACHING SERIES

DREAMS AND VISIONS

Lesson 4

DREAMS AND VISIONS IN HISTORY

INTRODUCTION

History abounds with stories of dreams and visions. God has never left His people without a vision of Himself and His will. History is marked with dreams and visions of supernatural importance. God has continually communicated with mankind through dreams and visions. Satan has occasionally counterfeited God's methods.

The Bible records 34 separate incidents of dreams. Twenty-two are listed in the Old Testament and 12 in the New Testament. Twenty-one people who had visions are recorded in the Bible.

READING

Proverbs 29:18, *Where there is no vision, the people perish: but he that keepeth the law, happy is he.*

1. **DREAMS AND VISIONS IN THE OLD TESTAMENT**

    A. Abraham

        There are no dreams or visions recorded before the Flood. These records begin with Abraham. God guided the life of Abraham with a vision. He commanded fear to leave Abraham; God was his shield or protector. God was his exceeding great Rewarder, Blesser, Helper, and Keeper.

        Genesis 15:1, *After these things the word of the LORD came unto Abram in a vision, saying, Fear not, Abram: I am thy shield, and thy exceeding great reward.*

    B. Jacob

        Jacob also had a vision. After he saw a ladder from earth to heaven with angels ascending and descending, Jacob was led and guided by the supernatural.

Genesis 46:2, *And God spake unto Israel in the visions of the night, and said, Jacob, Jacob. And he said, Here am I.*

C. Joseph

Joseph, the son of Jacob, was the 11th son in a large family. No one expected him to be any different from his brothers.

He had two dreams when he was 17 years old. They changed his life and directed his destiny.

Genesis 37:8-9, *And his brethren said to him, Shalt thou indeed reign over us? or shalt thou indeed have dominion over us? And they hated him yet the more for his dreams, and for his words.*
v. 9, *And he dreamed yet another dream, and told it his brethren, and said, Behold, I have dreamed a dream more; and, behold, the sun and the moon and the eleven stars made obeisance to me.*

D. The Egyptian Pharaoh

The Pharaoh of Egypt had a dream that he could not interpret, but God gave the interpretation to Joseph.

Genesis 41:17-21, *And Pharaoh said unto Joseph, In my dream, behold, I stood upon the bank of the river:*
v. 18, *And, behold, there came up out of the river seven kine, fat fleshed and well favored; and they fed in a meadow:*
v. 19, *And, behold, seven other kine came up after them, poor and very ill favored and lean fleshed, such as I never saw in all the land of Egypt for badness:*
v. 20, *And the lean and the ill favored kine did eat up the first seven fat kine:*
v. 21, *And when they had eaten them up, it could not be known that they had eaten them; but they were still ill favored, as at the beginning. So I awoke.*

E. Balaam

The prophet Balaam spoke about being in a trance.

Numbers 24:4-6, 15-16, *He hath said, which heard the words of God, which saw the vision of the Almighty, falling into a trance, but having his eyes open:*
v. 5, *How goodly are thy tents, O Jacob, and thy tabernacles, O Israel!*
v. 6, *As the valleys are they spread forth, as gardens by the river's side....*

v. 15, *And he took up his parable, and said, Balaam the son of Beor hath said, and the man whose eyes are open hath said:*

v. 16, *He hath said, which heard the word of God, and knew the knowledge of the most High, which saw the vision of the Almighty, falling into a trance, but having his eyes open.*

F. Samuel the prophet

Samuel had a vision as a small boy.

I Samuel 3:1-15, *And the child Samuel ministered unto the LORD before Eli. And the word of the LORD was precious in those days; there was no open vision.*
v. 2, *And it came to pass at that time, when Eli was laid down in his place, and his eyes began to wax dim, that he could not see;*
v. 3, *And ere the lamp of God went out in the temple of the LORD, where the ark of God was, and Samuel was laid down to sleep;*
v. 4, *That the LORD called Samuel: and he answered, Here am I.*
v. 5, *And he ran unto Eli, and said, Here am I; for thou calledst me. And he said, I called not; lie down again. And he went and lay down.*
v. 6, *And the LORD called yet again, Samuel. And Samuel arose and went to Eli, and said, Here am I; for thou didst call me. And he answered, I called not, my son; lie down again.*
v. 7, *Now Samuel did not yet know the LORD, neither was the word of the LORD yet revealed unto him.*
v. 8, *And the LORD called Samuel again the third time. And he arose and went to Eli, and said, Here am I; for thou didst call me. And Eli perceived that the LORD had called the child.*
v. 9, *Therefore Eli said unto Samuel, Go, lie down: and it shall be, if he call thee, that thou shalt say, Speak, LORD; for thy servant heareth. So Samuel went and lay down in his place.*
v. 10, *And the LORD came, and stood, and called as at other times, Samuel, Samuel. Then Samuel answered, Speak; for thy servant heareth.*
v. 11, *And the LORD said to Samuel, Behold, I will do a thing in Israel, at which both the ears of every one that heareth it shall tingle.*
v. 12, *In that day I will perform against Eli all things which I have spoken concerning his house: when I begin, I will also make an end.*
v. 13, *For I have told him that I will judge his house for ever for the iniquity which he knoweth; because his sons made themselves vile, and he restrained them not.*
v. 14, *And therefore I have sworn unto the house of Eli, that the iniquity of Eli's house shall not be purged with sacrifice nor offering for ever.*
v. 15, *And Samuel lay until the morning, and opened the doors of the house of the LORD. And Samuel feared to show Eli the vision.*

The record of a change of leadership in Israel is written here.

G. The prophet Isaiah

Isaiah prophesied from approximately 792 B.C. to 722 B.C.

The proper title for the writings of the great prophet, Isaiah, is found in the first chapter and first verse of the book of Isaiah.

Isaiah 1:1, *The vision of Isaiah the son of Amoz, which he saw concerning Judah and Jerusalem in the days of Uzziah, Jotham, Ahaz, and Hezekiah, kings of Judah.*

H. Jeremiah

Jeremiah 1:11-12, *Moreover the word of the LORD came unto me, saying, Jeremiah, what seest thou? And I said, I see a rod of an almond tree.*
v. 12, *Then said the LORD unto me, Thou hast well seen: for I will hasten my word to perform it.*

Over 100 years after Isaiah, Israel was blessed with another great seer. Jeremiah lived and prophesied from 685 B.C. to 616 B.C. He was a truly great man.

I. Ezekiel the prophet

1) Ezekiel 1:1, *Now it came to pass in the thirtieth year, in the fourth month, in the fifth day of the month, as I was among the captives by the river of Chebar, that the heavens were opened, and I saw visions of God.*

2) Ezekiel 8:1-4, 13, *And it came to pass in the sixth year, in the sixth month, in the fifth day of the month, as I sat in mine house, and the elders of Judah sat before me, that the hand of the Lord GOD fell there upon me.*
v. 2, *Then I beheld, and lo a likeness as the appearance of fire: from the appearance of his loins even downward, fire; and from his loins even upward, as the appearance of brightness, as the color of amber.*
v. 3, *And he put forth the form of an hand, and took me by a lock of mine head; and the spirit lifted me up between the earth and the heaven, and brought me in the visions of God to Jerusalem, to the door of the inner gate that looketh toward the north; where was the seat of the image of jealousy, which provoketh to jealousy.*
v. 4, *And, behold, the glory of the God of Israel was there, according to the vision that I saw in the plain.*

v. 13, *He said also unto me, Turn thee yet again, and thou shalt see greater abominations that they do.*

3) Ezekiel 11:24, *Afterwards the spirit took me up, and brought me in a vision by the Spirit of God into Chaldea, to them of the captivity. So the vision that I had seen went up from me.*

This was written from 622 B.C. to 600 B.C. in Babylon.

J. Daniel

The book of Daniel extends from 606 B.C. to 536 B.C. Some of the most remarkable dreams of history are recorded.

1) Daniel 2:19, *Then was the secret revealed unto Daniel in a night vision. Then Daniel blessed the God of heaven.*

2) Daniel 9:21-24, *Yea, whiles I was speaking in prayer, even the man Gabriel, whom I had seen in the vision at the beginning, being caused to fly swiftly, touched me about the time of the evening oblation.*
v. 22, And he informed me, and talked with me, and said, O Daniel, I am now come forth to give thee skill and understanding.
v. 23, At the beginning of thy supplications the commandment came forth, and I am come to show thee; for thou art greatly beloved: therefore understand the matter, and consider the vision.
v. 24, Seventy weeks are determined upon thy people and upon thy holy city, to finish the transgression, and to make an end of sins, and to make reconciliation for iniquity, and to bring in everlasting righteousness, and to seal up the vision and prophecy, and to anoint the most Holy.

K. Nebuchadnezzar, the king of Babylon

1) Emperors, monarchs and kings have had dreams that changed the course of history.

King Nebuchadnezzar, builder of the fabulous Babylonian Empire, saw or dreamt about the entire world system of Gentile government from the first empire, over which he ruled, to the ultimate empire of iron and clay. He saw all of the human world government smashed and disintegrated by a stone, cut without hands.

According to Daniel chapter 2, Nebuchadnezzar had this dream two years after he began his reign.

The Bible says the dream troubled him so much that he commanded all of his magicians, astrologers, sorcerers and Chaldeans to appear before him. He was greatly troubled by his dream but had forgotten it. The bewildered disciples of the

Devil, with their incantations and magic, were greatly troubled explaining it to the emperor.

Daniel 2:10-11, *The Chaldeans answered before the king, and said, There is not a man upon the earth that can show the king's matter: therefore there is no king, lord, nor ruler, that asked such things at any magician, or astrologer, or Chaldean.*
v. 11, *And it is a rare thing that the king requireth, and there is none other that can show it before the king, except the gods, whose dwelling is not with flesh.*

2) Since the first Gentile empire, there have been dreamers and interpreters of dreams.

King Nebuchadnezzar became exceedingly angry and demanded that all the magicians, astrologers and sorcerers in Babylon be killed if they could not recall his forgotten dream.

Daniel, a man of God, saved the wise men of King Nebuchadnezzar.

Daniel 2:19-23, *Then was the secret revealed unto Daniel in a night vision. Then Daniel blessed the God of heaven.*
v. 20, *Daniel answered and said, Blessed be the name of God for ever and ever: for wisdom and might are his:*
v. 21, *And he changeth the times and the seasons: he removeth kings, and setteth up kings: he giveth wisdom unto the wise, and knowledge to them that know understanding:*
v. 22, *He revealeth the deep and secret things: he knoweth what is in the darkness, and the light dwelleth with him.*
v. 23, *I thank thee, and praise thee, O thou God of my fathers, who hast given me wisdom and might, and hast made known unto me now what we desired of thee: for thou hast now made known unto us the king's matter.*

3) The king's dream

King Nebuchadnezzar dreamt the vision of the great image of world empires with a head of gold, breast and arms of silver, his belly and thighs of brass, his legs of iron and his feet part of iron and part of clay. Daniel told the king that the image was great and that he represented the head of gold, the brightest and richest of all empires.

Daniel's remarkable description of the world empires shook the royal ruler.

Daniel 2:46-48, *Then the king Nebuchadnezzar fell upon his face, and worshipped*

Daniel, and commanded that they should offer an oblation and sweet odors unto him.
v. 47, *The king answered unto Daniel, and said, Of a truth it is, that your God is a God of gods, and a Lord of kings, and a revealer of secrets, seeing thou couldest reveal this secret.*
v. 48, *Then the king made Daniel a great man, and gave him many great gifts, and made him ruler over the whole province of Babylon, and chief of the governors over all the wise men of Babylon.*

4)   King Nebuchadnezzar dreamt again.

In Daniel 4, King Nebuchadnezzar sent messages to all people, nations and languages on the earth. The message was related to the high God.

Daniel 4:3, 5, 7, 10, 12-14, 16, *How great are his signs! and how mighty are his wonders! his kingdom is an everlasting kingdom, and his dominion is from generation to generation.*

v. 5, *I saw a dream which made me afraid, and the thoughts upon my bed and the visions of my head troubled me.*

v. 7, *Then came in the magicians, the astrologers, the Chaldeans, and the soothsayers: and I told the dream before them; but they did not make known unto me the interpretation thereof.*

v. 10, *Thus were the visions of mine head in my bed; I saw, and behold, a tree in the midst of the earth, and the height thereof was great.*

v. 12, *The leaves thereof were fair, and the fruit thereof much, and in it was meat for all: the beasts of the field had shadow under it, and the fowls of the heaven dwelt in the boughs thereof, and all flesh was fed of it.*
v. 13, *I saw in the visions of my head upon my bed, and, behold, a watcher and an holy one came down from heaven;*
v. 14, *He cried aloud, and said thus, Hew down the tree, and cut off his branches, shake off his leaves, and scatter his fruit: let the beasts get away from under it, and the fowls from his branches:*

v. 16, *Let his heart be changed from man's, and let a beast's heart be given unto him: and let seven times pass over him.*

Again the king pled with Daniel to tell him what the dream meant.

Daniel 4:19, 22, 25, 27, *Then Daniel, whose name was Belteshazzar, was astonied for one hour, and his thoughts troubled him. The king spake, and said, Belteshazzar, let not the dream, or the interpretation thereof, trouble thee. Belteshazzar answered and said, My lord, the dream be to them that hate thee, and the interpretation thereof to thine enemies.*

v. 22, *It is thou, O king, that art grown and become strong: for thy greatness is grown, and reacheth unto heaven, and thy dominion to the end of the earth.*

v. 25, *That they shall drive thee from men, and thy dwelling shall be with the beasts of the field, and they shall make thee to eat grass as oxen, and they shall wet thee with the dew of heaven, and seven times shall pass over thee, till thou know that the most High ruleth in the kingdom of men, and giveth it to whomsoever he will.*

v. 27, *Wherefore, O king, let my counsel be acceptable unto thee, and break off thy sins by righteousness, and thine iniquities by showing mercy to the poor; if it may be a lengthening of thy tranquillity.*

Exactly one year later the king became a wild maniac. He was walking in the palace of the great Babylonian Empire, built by the power of his might, when he heard a voice from heaven that spelled his destiny.

Daniel 4:31-33, *While the word was in the king's mouth, there fell a voice from heaven, saying, O king Nebuchadnezzar, to thee it is spoken; The kingdom is departed from thee.*
v. 32, *And they shall drive thee from men, and thy dwelling shall be with the beasts of the field: they shall make thee to eat grass as oxen, and seven times shall pass over thee, until thou know that the most High ruleth in the kingdom of men, and giveth it to whomsoever he will.*
v. 33, *The same hour was the thing fulfilled upon Nebuchadnezzar: and he was driven from men, and did eat grass as oxen, and his body was wet with the dew of heaven, till his hairs were grown like eagles' feathers, and his nails like birds' claws.*

After the seven years the king was restored to his throne. The last we read of this king is in chapter 4.

Daniel 4:37, *Now I Nebuchadnezzar praise and extol and honor the King of heaven, all whose works are truth, and his ways judgment: and those that walk in pride he is able to abase.*

This is the end of the dreams of the emperor.

L. Habakkuk the prophet

Habakkuk 2:2-3, *And the LORD answered me, and said, Write the vision, and make it plain upon tables, that he may run that readeth it.*
v. 3, *For the vision is yet for an appointed time, but at the end it shall speak, and not lie: though it tarry, wait for it; because it will surely come, it will not tarry.*

M. Zechariah

The book of Zechariah was written between 557 B.C. to 525 B.C.

Zechariah 6:1, *And I turned, and lifted up mine eyes, and looked, and, behold, there came four chariots out from between two mountains; and the mountains were mountains of brass.*

N. The prophet Malachi

Malachi, the closing seer of the Old Testament, wrote from 557 B.C. to 525 B.C.

Malachi 1:1, *The burden of the word of the LORD to Israel by Malachi.*

2. DREAMS AND VISIONS IN THE NEW TESTAMENT

A. Zacharias and the birth of John the Baptist

Luke 1:22, *And when he came out, he could not speak unto them: and they perceived that he had seen a vision in the temple: for he beckoned unto them, and remained speechless.*

B. Jesus, James, Peter and John

Jesus and His disciples James, Peter and John experienced a vision on Mount Tabor.

Matthew 17:9, *And as they came down from the mountain, Jesus charged them, saying, Tell the vision to no man, until the Son of man be risen again from the dead.*

C. Peter

The Christian church turned to its world-wide mission because of a vision from God.

Acts 10:19, *While Peter thought on the vision, the Spirit said unto him, Behold, three men seek thee.*

D. Cornelius, the Roman Centurion

Acts 10:3-17, *He saw in a vision evidently about the ninth hour of the day an angel of God coming in to him, and saying unto him, Cornelius.*
v. 4, *And when he looked on him, he was afraid, and said, What is it, Lord? And he said unto him, Thy prayers and thine alms are come up for a memorial before God.*
v. 5, *And now send men to Joppa, and call for one Simon, whose surname is Peter:*
v. 6, *He lodgeth with one Simon a tanner, whose house is by the sea side: he shall tell thee what thou oughtest to do.*
v. 7, *And when the angel which spake unto Cornelius was departed, he called two of his household servants, and a devout soldier of them that waited on him continually;*
v. 8, *And when he had declared all these things unto them, he sent them to Joppa.*
v. 9, *On the morrow, as they went on their journey, and drew nigh unto the city, Peter went up upon the housetop to pray about the sixth hour:*
v. 10, *And he became very hungry, and would have eaten: but while they made ready, he fell into a trance,*
v. 11, *And saw heaven opened, and a certain vessel descending unto him, as it had been a great sheet knit at the four corners, and let down to the earth:*
v. 12, *Wherein were all manner of four-footed beasts of the earth, and wild beasts, and creeping things, and fowls of the air.*
v. 13, *And there came a voice to him, Rise, Peter; kill, and eat.*
v. 14, *But Peter said, Not so, Lord; for I have never eaten any thing that is common or unclean.*
v. 15, *And the voice spake unto him again the second time, What God hath cleansed, that call not thou common.*
v. 16, *This was done thrice: and the vessel was received up again into heaven.*
v. 17, *Now while Peter doubted in himself what this vision which he had seen should mean, behold, the men which were sent from Cornelius had made inquiry for Simon's house, and stood before the gate,*

E. A disciple named Ananias

Acts 9:10-12, *And there was a certain disciple at Damascus, named Ananias; and to him said the Lord in a vision, Ananias. And he said, Behold, I am here, Lord.*
v. 11, *And the Lord said unto him, Arise, and go into the street which is called Straight, and inquire in the house of Judas for one called Saul, of Tarsus: for, behold, he prayeth,*
v. 12, *And hath seen in a vision a man named Ananias coming in, and putting his hand on him, that he might receive his sight.*

F. Paul

1) Acts 16:9-10, *And a vision appeared to Paul in the night; There stood a man of Macedonia, and prayed him, saying, Come over into Macedonia, and help us.*

v. 10, *And after he had seen the vision, immediately we endeavored to go into Macedonia, assuredly gathering that the Lord had called us for to preach the gospel unto them.*

2) Acts 18:9, *Then spake the Lord to Paul in the night by a vision, Be not afraid, but speak, and hold not thy peace:*

3) II Corinthians 12:1-9, *It is not expedient for me doubtless to glory. I will come to visions and revelations of the Lord.*
   v. 2, *I knew a man in Christ above fourteen years ago, (whether in the body, I cannot tell; or whether out of the body, I cannot tell: God knoweth;) such an one caught up to the third heaven.*
   v. 3, *And I knew such a man, (whether in the body, or out of the body, I cannot tell: God knoweth;)*
   v. 4, *How that he was caught up into paradise, and heard unspeakable words, which it is not lawful for a man to utter.*
   v. 5, *Of such an one will I glory: yet of myself I will not glory, but in mine infirmities.*
   v. 6, *For though I would desire to glory, I shall not be a fool; for I will say the truth: but now I forbear, lest any man should think of me above that which he seeth me to be, or that he heareth of me.*
   v. 7, *And lest I should be exalted above measure through the abundance of the revelations, there was given to me a thorn in the flesh, the messenger of Satan to buffet me, lest I should be exalted above measure.*
   v. 8, *For this thing I besought the Lord thrice, that it might depart from me.*
   v. 9, *And he said unto me, My grace is sufficient for thee: for my strength is made perfect in weakness. Most gladly therefore will I rather glory in my infirmities, that the power of Christ may rest upon me.*

G. John, the beloved

Revelation 9:17, *And thus I saw the horses in the vision, and them that sat on them, having breastplates of fire, and of jacinth, and brimstone: and the heads of the horses were as the heads of lions; and out of their mouths issued fire and smoke and brimstone.*

STUDY GUIDE

LESTER SUMRALL TEACHING SERIES

DREAMS AND VISIONS

Lesson 5

WHO CAN HAVE DREAMS AND VISIONS?

INTRODUCTION

In the Word of God, male and female, young and old have experienced dreams, visions and trances. God does not regard individuals. Whoever opens his or her heart to Him can be rewarded with the supernatural.

Dreams and visions can come to those who are famous or small in prestige or insignificant to society.

READING:

Joel 2:28, *And it shall come to pass afterward, that I will pour out my spirit upon all flesh; and your sons and your daughters shall prophesy, your old men shall dream dreams, your young men shall see visions.*

1. **TO THE YOUNG AND THE OLD**

   Isaiah 44:3, *For I will pour water upon him that is thirsty, and floods upon the dry ground: I will pour my spirit upon thy seed, and my blessing upon thine offspring:*

2. **PROPHECY OF THE LAST DAYS**

   Acts 2:17-18, *And it shall come to pass in the last days, saith God, I will pour out of my Spirit upon all flesh: and your sons and your daughters shall prophesy, and your young men shall see visions, and your old men shall dream dreams:*
   v. 18, *And on my servants and on my handmaidens I will pour out in those days of my Spirit; and they shall prophesy:*

   The apostle Peter proclaimed in Acts 2:17-18:

   A. *And it shall come to pass in the last days…* Time

B. *I will pour out of my Spirit*...God's Spirit, the Holy Spirit

C. *Upon all flesh*... Scope

D. *Your sons and your daughters*...Both male and female

E. *Shall prophesy*...They will not preach a dead theology

F. *Your young men*...The changing of the guard! Youth aflame

G. *Shall see visions*...Strong eyes will behold the future, and see great accomplishments performed. These accomplishments will be performed by people of strength, courage and faith.

H. *Your old men*...The mature, well trained, and experienced

I. *Shall dream dreams*...The past will be revealed; both God's love and His judgment.

J. Today's fulfillment:

Earth is revisited with tremendous revival, revealed by visions and dreams.

The old are not too old.

The young are not too young.

There is no generation gap. There is unity. There is union. There is strength and judgment.

3. A PRESIDENT DREAMS

Carl Sandburg related a story about a dream that Abraham Lincoln had a few weeks before he died.

> "About ten days ago," said he [Abraham Lincoln], "I retired very late. I had been up waiting for important dispatches from the front. I could not have been long in bed when I fell into a slumber, for I was very weary. I soon began to dream. There seemed to be a death-like stillness about me. Then I heard subdued sobs, as if a number of people were weeping. I thought I left my bed and wandered downstairs. There the silence was broken by the same pitiful sobbing, but the mourners were invisible. I went from room to room; no living person was in sight, but the same mournful sounds of distress met me as I passed along. It was light in all the rooms; every object was familiar to me; but where were all the people who were grieving as if their hearts would

break? I was puzzled and alarmed. What could be the meaning of all this? Determined to find the cause of a state of things so mysterious and so shocking, I kept on until I arrived at the East Room, which I entered. There I met with a sickening surprise. Before me was a catafalque, on which rested a corpse wrapped in funeral vestments. Around it were stationed soldiers who were acting as guard; and there was a throng of people, some gazing mournfully upon the corpse, whose face was covered, others weeping pitifully. 'Who is dead in the White House?' I demanded of one of the soldiers. 'The President,' was his answer; 'he was killed by an assassin!' Then came a loud burst of grief from the crowd, which awoke me from my dream. I slept no more that night; and although it was only a dream, I have been strangely annoyed by it ever since."[1]

They replied, "The President is dead?" Then he walked over and saw himself in the casket.

This dream came as a warning to him to be extra careful about his protection. It was the lack of protection which caused his death.

4. THE VISIONS OF JOAN OF ARC

Joan of Arc was born around 1412 in France. She had a vision that she was chosen to liberate France from the British.

When she was about 17, Joan led the armies of King Charles VII of France into battle against the English at Orleans in 1429. She also brilliantly led the armies of France to the city of Reims.

Joan of Arc was captured by certain Frenchmen from Burgundy and sold to the British. She was burned at the stake in Rouen on May 30, 1431 at 19 years of age.

In 1920 she was canonized as a saint of the Catholic church.

5. LORD ALFRED TENNYSON

In 1842, Lord Alfred Tennyson had a remarkable vision. He related this vision in his poem, *A Poet's Prophecy*:

For I dipt into the future, far as human eye could see,
Saw the Vision of the world, and all the wonder that would be;

---

[1] Sandburg, Carl. <u>Abraham Lincoln: The War Years, Vol. 4</u>. (New York: Harcourt, Brace and Company, 1939), pp. 244-245.

> Saw the heavens fill with commerce, argosies of magic sails,
> Pilots of the purple twilight, dropping down with costly bales;
> Heard the heavens fill with shouting, and there rained a ghastly dew
> From the nations' airy navies grappling in the central blue;
> Far along the world-wide whisper of the south-wind rushing warm,
> With the standards of the peoples plunging through the thunderstorm;
> Till the war-drum throbb'd no longer, and the battle flags were furl'd
> In the Parliament of man, the Federation of the world.
> There the common sense of most shall hold a fretful realm in awe,
> And the kindly earth shall slumber, lapt in universal law.[2]

Before there were airplanes, Lord Alfred Tennyson saw them.

He heard the sky fighting and saw the poison rain and dew.

He saw a Parliament of men and Federation of the world—the one-world Antichrist system.

6. THE ROLAND BUCK STORY

Charles and Frances Hunter published the story of Pastor Roland Buck's encounters with angels. Here are excerpts from this book, <u>Angels on Assignment</u>.

> ...just after I had gone to bed, I noticed a bluish glow coming from the staircase. I knew it was too dim to be the light for the staircase so I thought that possibly I had left a light on in one of the downstairs rooms. I got up, and started down to turn the light off.

> I was halfway down the stairs when the light flipped on! Standing before me were two of the largest men I had ever seen in my life! I was shocked! I wasn't exactly frightened, but there was such a radiation of divine power which comes from them dwelling in the brightness of God's presence that I could not stand up! My knees buckled and I started to fall! One of the huge beings reached out, took hold of me, and my strength returned.

> He very simply told me he was the angel Gabriel![3]

> ...during the two to four hours they have stayed each time they have come, there has not been one verse of Scripture quoted. Instead, a living panorama causes truth to literally come alive as it passes before me. At times I have

---

[2] Tennyson, Lord Alfred. "A Poet's Prophecy," <u>Poems Teachers Ask For Book One</u>. (Dansville, NY: F. A. Owen Publishing Company, no date), p. 1.

[3] Hunter, Charles and Frances. <u>Angels on Assignment</u>. (Kingwood, TX: Hunter Books, 1979), p. 39.

found myself living what I was seeing. Not once did they leave without giving Bible references where the message could be found.[4]

7. WOMEN WILL SEE VISIONS AND DREAM DREAMS

A. Eve saw a manifestation of Satan in the serpent.

Genesis 3:2, 4, 13, *And the woman said unto the serpent, We may eat of the fruit of the trees of the garden:*

v. 4, *And the serpent said unto the woman, Ye shall not surely die:*

v. 13, *And the LORD God said unto the woman, What is this that thou hast done? And the woman said, The serpent beguiled me, and I did eat.*

B. Sarah saw a manifestation of God and served food to Him and the angels who destroyed Sodom and Gomorrah.

Genesis 18:1-2, 9-10, *And the LORD appeared unto him in the plains of Mamre: and he sat in the tent door in the heat of the day;*
v. 2, *And he lift up his eyes and looked, and, lo, three men stood by him: and when he saw them, he ran to meet them from the tent door, and bowed himself toward the ground,*

v. 9, *And they said unto him, Where is Sarah thy wife? And he said, Behold, in the tent.*
v. 10, *And he said, I will certainly return unto thee according to the time of life; and, lo, Sarah thy wife shall have a son. And Sarah heard it in the tent door, which was behind him.*

C. The witch of Endor called up an image of Samuel who had deceased. She saw it and was frightened.

I Samuel 28:7, 13-14, *Then said Saul unto his servants, Seek me a woman that hath a familiar spirit, that I may go to her, and inquire of her. And his servants said to him, Behold, there is a woman that hath a familiar spirit at Endor.*

v. 13, *And the king said unto her, Be not afraid: for what sawest thou? And the woman said unto Saul, I saw gods ascending out of the earth.*
v. 14, *And he said unto her, What form is he of? And she said, An old man cometh up; and he is covered with a mantle. And Saul perceived that it was Samuel, and he stooped with his face to the ground, and bowed himself.*

---

[4] Hunter, p. 14.

D. Mary Magdalene saw and spoke to a vision of angels.

Luke 24:23, *And when they found not his body, they came, saying, that they had also seen a vision of angels, which said that he was alive.*

E. The Virgin Mary saw an angel.

Luke 1:28-33, *And the angel came in unto her, and said, Hail, thou that art highly favored, the Lord is with thee: blessed art thou among women.*
v. 29, And when she saw him, she was troubled at his saying, and cast in her mind what manner of salutation this should be.
v. 30, And the angel said unto her, Fear not, Mary: for thou hast found favor with God.
v. 31, And, behold, thou shalt conceive in thy womb, and bring forth a son, and shalt call his name JESUS.
v. 32, He shall be great, and shall be called the Son of the Highest: and the Lord God shall give unto him the throne of his father David:
v. 33, And he shall reign over the house of Jacob for ever; and of his kingdom there shall be no end.

F. Pilate's wife

1) Pilate's wife only entrance into history was when she had a dream.

Matthew 27:19, *When he was set down on the judgment seat, his wife sent unto him, saying, Have thou nothing to do with that just man: for I have suffered many things this day in a dream because of him.*

2) The massive public resistance to justice overwhelmed the message from his wife.

Matthew 27:20, 24, *But the chief priests and elders persuaded the multitude that they should ask Barabbas, and destroy Jesus.*

v. 24, *When Pilate saw that he could prevail nothing, but that rather a tumult was made, he took water, and washed his hands before the multitude, saying, I am innocent of the blood of this just person: see ye to it.*

G. My mother dreamed.

When I was about eight or ten years old, my mother had a cancer in her breast. It was a lump about the size of a silver dollar and went deep into her flesh. The doctors dressed the open sore and were afraid that surgery would bring early death. It was so painful that she often wept.

One night my mother dreamed that Jesus entered her room. He stood at the foot of her bed and touched her with His finger. The next morning she told my father.

In three or four days when my father asked her how the cancer was, she responded, "The pain is gone." She removed the bandage and gauze. There lay the cancer with its tendrils in the cotton! New skin had grown over the hole.

My mother lived more than 45 years after that and never again had a problem with breast cancer.

H. My mother and the stranger.

A man came to the door asking for food. After he finished eating and went out the door, she immediately went looking for him because there was something strange about him. She could not find him, and she felt that she possibly had fed an angel.

I. Female witch in the Philippines.

I was dedicating a church that I had built among some tribes, and a head witchdoctor fought it. She came to the meeting and made strange noises, trying to break up the meeting. I did not know that she was a witch, but when she stood up I commanded her to sit down and cease to speak.

The next day when we left the tribe, she still had not been able to say a word.

_____

_____

_____

_____

_____

_____

_____

_____

_____

_____

_____

_____

_____

_____

_____

_____

_____

_____

STUDY GUIDE

LESTER SUMRALL TEACHING SERIES

DREAMS AND VISIONS

Lesson 6

AMERICA'S FIRST PRESIDENT SAW A PROPHETIC VISION

INTRODUCTION

George Washington, the first President of the United States, had a vision of the future of America, including its wars.

There are several versions of the vision. I have two. Some believe the vision to be a legend. The offices of Mt. Vernon, George Washington's home in Virginia, have sent me considerable information about it. The version of the vision in this lesson is taken from Gordon Lindsay's book, Will Our President Die in Office?

READING

Daniel 7:15, *I Daniel was grieved in my spirit in the midst of my body, and the visions of my head troubled me.*
v. 16, *I came near unto one of them that stood by, and asked him the truth of all this. So he told me, and made me know the interpretation of the things.*

The details of the vision were communicated to Professor Totten by Anthony Sherman, who was with George Washington at Valley Forge.[1]

The Vision

One day [at Valley Forge], I remember it well, the chilly winds whistled through the leafless trees, and though the sky was cloudless and the sun shone brightly, he [George Washington] remained in his quarters nearly all the afternoon alone. When he came out I noticed his face was a shade paler than usual, and there seemed to be something on his mind of more than

---

[1] Gordon Lindsay, Will Our President Die in Office? (Dallas: Christ For the Nations, 1980), p. 67.

ordinary importance. Returning just after dusk he dispatched an orderly to the quarters of the officer…who was in attendance. After a preliminary conversation of about a half hour, Washington gazing upon his companion with a strange look of dignity which he alone could command, said to the latter:

'I do not know whether it is owing to the anxiety of my mind, or what, but this afternoon as I was sitting at this very table engaged in preparing a dispatch, something in the apartment seemed to disturb me. Looking up, I beheld standing opposite me a singularly beautiful female. So astonished was I, for I had given strict orders not to be disturbed, it was some moments before I found language to inquire the cause of her presence. A second, a third, and even a fourth time, did I repeat my question, but received no answer from my mysterious visitor except a slight raising of the eyes. By this time I felt strange sensations spreading through me. I would have risen, but the riveted gaze of the being before me rendered volition impossible. I essayed once more to address her, but my tongue had become powerless. Even thought itself suddenly became paralyzed. A new influence, mysterious, potent, irresistible, took possession of me. All I could do was to gaze steadily, vacantly, at my unknown visitant. Gradually the surrounding atmosphere seemed as though it became filled with sensations, and grew luminous. Everything about me seemed to rarefy, the mysterious visitor herself becoming more airy, and yet more distinct to my sight than before. I now began to feel as one dying, or rather to experience the sensations which I have sometimes imagined accompany dissolution. I did not think, I did not reason, I did not move—all were alike impossible. I was only conscious of gazing fixedly, vacantly at my companion.'

The War of 1812

'Presently I heard a voice saying, "Son of the Republic, look and learn." At the same time my visitor extended her arm eastward. I now beheld a heavy white vapor at some distance rising fold upon fold. This gradually dissipated, and I looked upon a strange scene. Before me lay Europe, Asia, Africa and America. I saw rolling and tossing between Europe and America the billows of the Atlantic, and between Asia and America lay the Pacific. "Son of the Republic," said the same voice as before, "look and learn." At that moment I beheld a dark shadowy being like an angel standing, or floating in midair between Europe and America. Dipping water out of the ocean in the hollow of each hand, he sprinkled some upon America with his right hand, while with his left hand he cast some on Europe. Immediately a dark cloud raised from these countries and joined in mid-ocean. For a while it remained stationary and then moved slowly westward, until it enveloped America in its murky folds. Sharp flashes of lightning gleamed through it at intervals, and I heard the groans and cries of the American people. A second time the angel dipped water from the ocean, and sprinkled it as before. The dark cloud was then drawn back to the ocean, in whose heaving billows it sank from view. A third time I heard the mysterious voice saying, "Son of the Republic, look and learn." I cast my eyes upon America and beheld villages and towns and cities springing up, one after another until the whole land from the Atlantic to the

Pacific was dotted with them. Again I heard the mysterious voice say, "Son of the Republic, the end of the century cometh; look and learn."'

The Civil War

'At this the dark, shadowy angel turned his face southward, and from Africa I saw an ill-omened specter approach our land. It flitted slowly and heavily over every town and city of the latter. The inhabitants presently set themselves in battle array against each other. As I continued looking, I saw a bright angel, on whose brow rested the word "Union," bearing the American flag, which he placed between the divided nation and said, "Remember ye are brethren." Instantly the inhabitants casting from them their weapons, became friends once more and united around the National Standard.'

World War III

'And again I heard the mysterious voice say, "Son of the Republic, look and learn." At this, the dark, shadowy angel placed a trumpet to his mouth and blew three blasts; and taking water from the ocean, he sprinkled it upon Europe, Asia and Africa. Then my eyes beheld a fearful scene: From each of these countries arose thick black clouds that were soon joined into one. Throughout this mass there gleamed a dark red light by which I saw hordes of armed men, who moved with the cloud, marching by land and sailing by sea to America, which country was enveloped in the volume of the cloud. And I dimly saw these vast armies devastate the whole country and burn the villages, towns and cities that I had beheld springing up. As my ears listened to the thundering of the cannon, clashing of swords and shouts and cries of millions in mortal combat, I again heard the mysterious voice saying, "Son of the Republic, look and learn." When the voice had ceased, the dark, shadowy angel placed his trumpet once more to his mouth and blew a loud and fearful blast.'

Final Victory for America

'Instantly a light as of a thousand suns shone down from above me and broke into fragments the dark cloud which enveloped America. At the same moment the angel upon whose head still shone the word "Union," and who bore our national flag in one hand and a sword in the other, descended from heaven attended by legions of bright spirits. These immediately joined the inhabitants of America, who, I perceived, were well nigh overcome, but who, immediately taking courage again, closed up their broken ranks and renewed the battle. Again amid the fearful noise of the conflict, I heard the mysterious voice saying, "Son of the Republic, look and learn." As the voice ceased, the shadowy angel for the last time dipped water from the ocean and sprinkled it upon America. Instantly the dark cloud rolled back, together with the armies it had brought, leaving the inhabitants of the land victorious.

'Then once more I beheld villages, towns and cities springing up where they had been before while the bright angel, planting the azure standard he had brought into the midst of them, cried with a loud voice: "While the stars remain and the heavens send down dew upon the earth, so long shall the Republic last." And taking from his brow the crown on which was emblazoned the word "Union," he placed it upon the standard while the people, kneeling down, said "Amen."

'The scene instantly began to fade and dissolve and I at last saw nothing but the rising, curling vapor I at first beheld. This also disappearing, I found myself once more gazing upon my mysterious visitor, who, in the same voice I had heard before said, "Son of the Republic, what you have seen is thus interpreted: Three great perils will come upon the Republic. The most fearful is the third, passing which, the whole world united shall not prevail against her. Let every child of the Republic learn to live for God, His land and union." With these words the vision vanished, and I started from my seat and felt that I had seen a vision wherein it had shown me the birth, progress and destiny of the United States."'[2]

---

[2] Lindsay, pp. 69-73.

_____

_____

_____

_____

_____

_____

_____

_____

_____

_____

_____

_____

_____

_____

_____

_____

_____

_____

_____

_____

_____

_____

STUDY GUIDE

LESTER SUMRALL TEACHING SERIES

DREAMS AND VISIONS

Lesson 7

THE GIANT WAS THE CHURCH:
A VISION OF THE CHURCH TODAY

INTRODUCTION

Tommy Hicks was a friend of mine for several years. He led, by the power of the Holy Spirit, the great Argentine Revival. God gave him a vision of the end times, and the prophetic end-time ministry.

READING:

Acts 2:17, *And it shall come to pass in the last days, saith God, I will pour out of my Spirit upon all flesh: and your sons and your daughters shall prophesy, and your young men shall see visions, and your old men shall dream dreams.*

1.   **INTRODUCING THE VISION**

Reverend Tommy Hicks said that this vision began July 25, 1961, at about 2:30 in the morning in Winnipeg, Canada. The vision came three times, with exactly the same detail, that morning. The following is how he related it to me.

The greatest time of the church is ahead of us.

I was so stirred and so moved by the revelation that this has changed my complete outlook upon the Body of Christ, and upon the end-time ministry. The greatest gifts that the Church of Jesus Christ has ever received lie ahead. It is difficult to help men and women to realize what God is trying to give to His people in the end times.

I did not fully realize, nor could I understand, the fullness of the vision until I read in the book of Joel:

Joel 2:23, *Be glad then, ye children of Zion, and rejoice in the LORD your God: for he hath given you the former rain moderately, and he will cause to come down for you the rain, the former rain, and the latter rain in the first month.*

Not only will God send the former and the latter rain, but He is going to give His people a double portion of the power of God in these last days.

2. THE VISION

When this vision appeared to me [Tommy Hicks], I suddenly found myself at a great height. I was looking down upon the earth, when suddenly the whole world came into view–every nation, every kindred, every tongue came into my line of sight. From the east and the west; north and the south; I recognized the countries and cities that I had been visited. I was nearly in fear and trembling as I stood beholding the great sight before me. At that moment when the world came into view, it began to lightning and thunder.

A. The Great Giant

As the lightning flashed over the face of the earth, my eyes went downward–I was facing north. Suddenly I beheld what looked like a great giant. As I stared at it, I was almost bewildered by the sight. The giant was gigantic. His feet seemed to reach to the North Pole and his head to the South Pole. His arms were stretched from sea to sea. I could not even begin to understand whether this was a mountain or a giant. As I watched, I realized that it was a great giant. I could see he was struggling for life, to even live. His body was covered with debris from head to foot; and at times this great giant would move his body and act as though he would rise up. When he did, thousands of little creatures seemed to run away. Hideous looking creatures would run away from this giant and when he became calm, they would come back.

B. The Giant Lifted Up

All of a sudden this great giant lifted one hand toward the heavens, and then he lifted his other hand. When he did, these creatures seemed to flee away from this giant by the thousands and to go out into the darkness and the night.

Slowly this great giant began to rise—as he did, his head and hands entered the clouds. As he rose to his feet, he seemed to have cleansed himself from the debris and filth that had been on him. He began to raise his hands into the heavens as though praising the Lord. As he raised his hands, they went into the clouds.

Suddenly every cloud became silver; the most beautiful silver that I have ever seen. As I watched the phenomenon, it was so great that I could not even begin to understand what it all meant. I was stirred as I watched it. I cried unto the Lord and I said, "Oh, Lord, what is the meaning of this?" Then I felt as if I were in the Spirit, and I could feel the presence of the Lord.

C. The Light of the Giant

Suddenly from the silver clouds came great drops of liquid light raining down upon this mighty giant. Slowly, slowly this giant began to melt—he began to sink into the very earth itself. As he melted, his whole form seemed to melt over the face of the earth. This great rain began to come down. Liquid drops of light began to flood the very earth itself. Suddenly this giant that seemed to melt became millions of people all over the face of the earth. As I beheld the sight before me, people stood up all over the world. They were lifting their hands and praising the Lord.

D. Great Thunder

At that moment a great thunder seemed to roar from the heavens. I turned my eyes toward the heavens, and suddenly I saw a figure in glistening white—the most glorious being I have ever seen in all my life. I did not see His face, but somehow I knew that it was the Lord Jesus Christ. He stretched forth His hand. He would stretch it forth to one, then to another, and to another. He continued to stretch forth His hand upon the peoples and the nations of the world—men and women. He pointed toward them and this same liquid light seemed to flow from His hand into people, and the mighty anointing of God came upon them. Those people then began to go forth in the name of the Lord.

E. Unwanted Anointing

I do not know how long I watched it. It seemed it went into days and weeks and months. I beheld Christ as He continued to stretch forth His hand, when a tragedy occurred. There were many people, when He stretched His hand toward them, who refused the anointing and the call of God. I saw men and women I knew, people that I felt certainly would received the call of God; but as He stretched forth His hand toward this one, or toward that one, they simply bowed their heads and began to back away. Each person who seemed to bow down and back away appeared to go into darkness. Blackness seemed to swallow them everywhere.

F. A New Army

I was bewildered as I watched. The people He had anointed covered the earth. There were hundreds of thousands of these people all over the world—in Africa, Asia, Russia, China, and America—all over the world. The anointing of God was upon these people as they went forth in the name of the Lord. I watched these people as they went. They were ditch diggers, washer women, rich men, and poor men. I saw people bound with paralysis, sickness, blindness and deafness. As the Lord stretched forth His hand to give them this anointing, they became well, they became healed—and they went forth!

This is the miracle of it—the glorious miracle of it! Those people would stretch forth their hands exactly as the Lord did, and it seemed that this same liquid was in their hands. As they stretched forth their hands, they said, "According to my word, be thou made whole."

As these people continued in their mighty end-time ministry, I did not fully realize what was happening. I looked to the Lord and said, "What is the meaning of this?" He said, "This is that which I will do in the last days. I will restore all that the cankerworm, the palmer-worm, and the caterpillar have destroyed. This, My people in the end time, shall go forth. As a mighty army they shall sweep over the face of the earth."

G. Spiritual Transportation

While I was at this great height, I could behold the whole world. I watched these people as they were going to and fro over the face of the earth. Suddenly a man from Africa would be transported in a moment by the Spirit of God to Russia, China, America, or some other place, and vice versa. These people went all over the world. They went through fire, pestilence, famine and persecution—nothing seemed to stop them.

H. Angry Mobs

Angry mobs came to these anointed ones with swords and guns. Like Jesus, they passed through the multitude, and could not be found. The consecrated ones went everywhere stretching forth their hands in the name of the Lord. When they did, the sick were healed and blind eyes were opened. There were no long prayers. I never saw a church, and I never saw or heard of any denomination. These people were out in the name of the Lord of hosts.

They marched forward as the ministry of Christ in the end time led them, and ministered to the multitudes over the face of the earth. Tens of thousands, even millions, seemed to come to the Lord Jesus Christ as these people gave the message of the coming kingdom. It was so glorious! There were those who rebelled and become angry. They tried to attack the workers that were giving the message.

I. God Moves

God is going to give the world a demonstration in this last hour such as has never been known before. These men and women came from all walks of life. Degrees will mean nothing. I saw these workers as they went over the face of the earth. When one would stumble and fall, another would come and pick him up. There was no big "I" and little "you" attitudes. Every mountain was brought low, and every valley was exalted. They seemed to have one thing in common—a divine love that seemed to flow from these people as they went together, worked together, and lived together. It was the theme of their lives. As the days went by, I stood and beheld this sight. I could only cry—and sometimes I laughed. It was so wonderful as these people went throughout the face of the whole earth showing forth God's power in this last end time.

J.   Liquid Light

As I watched from the very heaven itself, there were times when great deluges of this liquid light seemed to fall upon great congregations. The congregations would lift their hands and praise God for what seemed like hours, and even days, as the Spirit of God came upon them. God said, "I will pour out My Spirit upon all flesh." That is exactly what God was doing. From every man and woman who received this power and anointing of God, the miracles of God flowed continuously.

K.   A Clap of Thunder—Rapture

Suddenly there was another great clap of thunder that seemed to resound around the world. Again I heard the voice saying, "Now, this is My people; this is My beloved bride." When the voice spoke, I looked upon the earth and I saw the lakes and the mountains. The graves were opened and people from all over the world, the saints of all ages, seemed to be rising. As they rose from the graves, suddenly all these people came from every direction—from the east and west, north and south. They seemed to be forming this gigantic body again. The dead in Christ seemed to rise first, but I could hardly comprehend it, it was so marvelous and far beyond anything I could ever dream or think of!

L.   A Giant Again

This huge body suddenly began to form and take shape, and its shape was again in the form of the mighty giant, but this time it was different. It was arrayed in beautiful, gorgeous white. Its garments were without spot or wrinkle as the body began to form, and the people of all ages seemed to be gathering into the body. Slowly, from the heavens above, the Lord Jesus came and became the head. I heard another clap of thunder that said, "This is My beloved bride for whom I have waited. She will come forth, even tried by fire. This is she whom I have loved from the beginning of time."

M.   The Fourth Voice—Great Tribulation

As I watched, my eyes turned to the far north and I saw great destruction, buildings being destroyed and men and women crying out in anguish. Then I heard a fourth voice that said, "Now is My wrath being poured out upon the face of the earth."

From the ends of the whole world, great vials of God's wrath were being poured out upon the face of the earth. I can remember it as I beheld the awful sight of cities and whole nations going down into destruction. I could hear weeping and the wailing. I could hear people crying. They seemed to cry as they went into caves, but the caves and the mountains opened up. They leaped into water, but the water would not drown them. There was nothing that could destroy them. Although they wanted to take their lives, they did not succeed.

N. I Returned to My Conscious Body

Again I turned my eyes toward the glorious sight of this body arrayed in the beautiful white shining garment. Slowly, slowly, it began to lift from the earth, and as it did, I awoke. The sight I had beheld was the end-time ministry of the church.

Again on July 27 at 2:30 in the morning the same revelation, the same vision, came once more exactly as it had before.

My life has changed as I realize that we are living in that end time. All over the world God is anointing men and women with this ministry. It will not be doctrine. It will not be "churchianity;" but it will be Jesus Christ. They will give forth the Word of the Lord and are going to say, as I heard so many times in the vision, "According to My word, it shall be done."

Oh people, listen to me! "According to My word, it shall be done." We will be clothed with the power and anointing of God!

We will not have to preach sermons.

We will not have to depend on man, nor will we be denominational echoes, but we will have the power of the living God!

We will fear no one, but will go forth in the name of the Lord of hosts!

Soon after this vision, Tommy Hicks died in Los Angeles, California, and went to be with the Lord. He was not permitted to see the fulfillment of his vision.

STUDY GUIDE

LESTER SUMRALL TEACHING SERIES

DREAMS AND VISIONS

Lesson 8

PERSONAL REALITY

INTRODUCTION

At two major turning points in my life, God has led me by a vision. Now over 60 years later, I can say with the apostle Paul, *I was not disobedient to the heavenly vision.*

My vision has not become dull with a lack of luster. My vision is not covered by something else. It has not been diluted, watered down, or compromised. My vision is not impaired or broken down. It is not torn, beaten, hurt or bleeding through mistreatment.

1. MY FIRST VISION

A. When I was 17 years old, I experienced my first supernatural vision.

I lay on my deathbed in our home in Panama City, Florida, slowly succumbing to the ravages of tuberculosis. One afternoon I started to choke and turn blue in the face. I had been spitting blood daily for weeks, but now I was hemorrhaging. "The boy is as good as dead," I heard the doctor tell my mother.

It is an awful feeling to know you are dying and you are not ready to die. I wanted to live. I wanted to be a businessman with goals of making a lot of money and becoming a great success.

For months Mother had been bringing in her "Prayer Meeting Group" to pray over me. They were persistent, standing around my bed, pleading with the Lord to spare my life, week after week. I asked Mother not to bring them back, but she did anyway.

B. This day was different. I was hovering between life and death, and I knew what was going on. My parents were crying. Then it happened.

On one side of my bed I saw a coffin, just my size, open and tilted. It was very pretty, but empty and waiting for me to die. I turned my head the other way. I did not want to look at that casket, but on the other side of my bed I saw a Bible. It reached from the floor to the ceiling. Then I heard God say, "That's My Word. You have a choice Lester, which of these will you choose tonight?"

It was not an audible voice, yet it was as distinct and as firm a voice as any I had ever heard. I did not want to be a preacher. Many times I had heard my mother sob, "Lord, save Lester and make him a preacher." I hated evangelists and had determined I was not going to be one of them.

C. I was fighting it out with God. I wanted to live, so I pleaded with God. "Lord, I'm afraid to die. I'm not ready to die. God, if the only way in the world for me to live is to preach—I will preach." I asked God to give me a long life of preaching and promised Him that I would never stop preaching as long as there was a breath in me.

It was settled. Just that quickly the vision vanished.

2. MY SECOND VISION

A. God changed the course of my life.

As a young man just starting out, after eighteen months of preaching, God miraculously changed the course of my ministry and my life. God gave me a vision of the world traveling on the Road of Life, the end of which was eternal destruction in a burning hell.

While I was sitting to the side of the pulpit in a little frame church building in the Tennessee countryside on December 18, 1931, I experienced this vision of an uncountable multitude of humankind traveling down a highway that ended abruptly at a precipice towering above a bottomless inferno. When this unending procession of people from every nation came to the end of the highway, I could see them falling off into eternity.

I was not aware of the people in that little church, the songs they were singing, or anything that was going on around me. I was only conscious of the screams of damned souls sinking into hell. In that vision, as God drew me nearer so I could see men and women plunging into that awful chasm, I saw their faces distorted with terror. I saw their hands flailing wildly, clawing at the air and each other.

B. You are responsible!

As I looked on in stunned silence, God spoke to me out of that frightening chaos, "You are responsible for these who are lost."

I backed away, crying out, "No, not me, Lord. I do not know these people. I have never been to Japan, the Philippines, China, or India. How can I be held responsible?"

66

The voice of the Lord was tender, yet firm.

When I say unto the wicked, Thou shalt surely die; and thou givest him not warning, nor speakest to warn the wicked from his wicked way, to save his life; the same wicked man shall die in his iniquity; but his blood will I require at thine hand.

I did not discover until later that this was a passage in the Bible, Ezekiel 3:18.

C. God left no doubt in my mind, showing me that I was responsible for turning a million souls from that road to the Road of Life that leads to the cross of Jesus Christ and to Christ Himself, who is the way of eternal life.

This vision made a world missionary out of me.

STUDY GUIDE

LESTER SUMRALL TEACHING SERIES

DREAMS AND VISIONS

Lesson 9

HOW TO PREPARE FOR SPIRITUAL DREAMS AND VISIONS

INTRODUCTION

Dreams and visions are still for today and you, too, can have spiritual dreams and visions.

READING:

Acts 2:39, *For the promise is unto you, and to your children, and to all that are afar off, even as many as the Lord our God shall call.*

1. **KNOW GOD, HIS LOVE, HIS POWER, AND HIS WORD**

   It is imperative to have a knowledge of God to have any spiritual revelation.

   A. Know God.

   I John 2:3-5, *And hereby we do know that we know him, if we keep his commandments.*
   v. 4, He that saith, I know him, and keepeth not his commandments, is a liar, and the truth is not in him.
   v. 5, But whoso keepeth his word, in him verily is the love of God perfected: hereby know we that we are in him.

   B. Know God's love.

   Ephesians 3:19, *And to know the love of Christ, which passeth knowledge, that ye might be filled with all the fullness of God.*

   C. Know God's power.

   Philippians 3:10, *That I may know him, and the power of his resurrection...*

D. Know God's Word.

Colossians 3:16, *Let the word of Christ dwell in you richly in all wisdom; teaching and admonishing one another in psalms and hymns and spiritual songs, singing with grace in your hearts to the Lord.*

2. BE WILLING

Do not pressure God. God can give revelation in His wisdom. You should be busy about activities close by. If God gives a further revelation, we can thank Him for it.

3. HAVE YOUR TOTAL LIFE COMMITTED TO GOD

God will not give great revelation or blessing to those who are not totally committed to Him. The people in the Bible who had revelation from God were those who had made strong commitments of dedication.

A. Abraham's commitment to God was severely tested when He was asked to offer up his son Isaac as a sacrifice.

Genesis 22:2, 12, *And he said, Take now thy son, thine only son Isaac, whom thou lovest, and get thee into the land of Moriah; and offer him there for a burnt offering upon one of the mountains which I will tell thee of.*

v. 12, *And he said, Lay not thine hand upon the lad, neither do thou any thing unto him: for now I know that thou fearest God, seeing thou hast not withheld thy son, thine only son from me.*

B. Joseph's commitment to God was tested when Potiphar's wife tempted him to commit fornication with her, but he refused.

Genesis 39:9, 17, 20, *There is none greater in this house than I; neither hath he kept back any thing from me but thee, because thou art his wife: how then can I do this great wickedness, and sin against God?*

v. 17, *And she spake unto him according to these words, saying, The Hebrew servant, which thou hast brought unto us, came in unto me to mock me:*

v. 20, *And Joseph's master took him, and put him into the prison, a place where the king's prisoners were bound: and he was there in the prison.*

4. BE WILLING TO COMMUNICATE TRUTH AND POWER

God always has a purpose. God is not selfish. He gives and He wishes the same spirit to be in His disciples. Believers must be willing to share whatever God gives to them with their fellow men.

5.   BE WILLING TO SERVE

The Word says that we are kings and priests. We must be as willing to receive orders as well as give them. We must be as willing to serve others as we are willing to be served.

A.   Matthew 25:37-40, *Then shall the righteous answer him, saying, Lord, when saw we thee an hungered, and fed thee? or thirsty, and gave thee drink?*
v. 38, *When saw we thee a stranger, and took thee in? or naked, and clothed thee?*
v. 39, *Or when saw we thee sick, or in prison, and came unto thee?*
v. 40, *And the King shall answer and say unto them, Verily I say unto you, Inasmuch as ye have done it unto one of the least of these my brethren, ye have done it unto me.*

B.   I Peter 2:9, *But ye are a chosen generation, a royal priesthood, an holy nation, a peculiar people; that ye should show forth the praises of him who hath called you out of darkness into his marvelous light:*

C.   Revelation 1:6, *And hath made us kings and priests unto God and his Father; to him be glory and dominion for ever and ever. Amen.*